CAYENNE PEPPER
The History. The Heat. The Health.

By Dr. Andrea Blake-Garrett

TABLE OF CONTENTS

To my cherished readers,

Your journey toward health and wellness is the cornerstone of these books. I am deeply honored that you've chosen to walk this path with me. Your commitment to learning, growing, and nurturing your well-being inspires every word I write. Thank you for your unwavering support and for sharing your honest reviews. Your feedback helps others discover these resources and fuels my passion to continue this important work. Together, we are building a stronger, healthier future. I am grateful beyond words for your trust and your voice.

Dominate YOUR Day!
With heartfelt appreciation,
Dr. ABG

INTRODUCTION

"If you master one herb in your life, master cayenne pepper. It is more powerful than any other." – Dr. Richard Shulze

As a little girl growing up on the island of Jamaica, I learned very early that spices have the remarkable ability to transform ordinary meals into extraordinary culinary experiences, igniting our body, our taste buds, and awakening our senses. Among the diverse array of spices that hold a special place in my grandmother's spice racks was one amazing spice. This spice stands out for its natural heat, explosive color, and undisputable ability to arouse passion: cayenne pepper.

Cayenne pepper, known the world of science as *Capsicum Annuum*, has a long and fascinating history that dates back thousands of years. From origins in Central and South America to its widespread use in homes, natural medicinal recipes and restaurants worldwide, cayenne pepper has left an undeniable mark on our health, culinary and cultural traditions.

The allure of cayenne pepper lies not only in its fiery heat but also in its diverse applications and verifiable health benefits. Throughout history, this spice has been revered for its ability to add depth, flavor, and a touch of heat to a wide range of dishes. From sizzling stir-fries to zesty sauces and spicy marinades, cayenne pepper has become an indispensable ingredient in kitchens worldwide.

Cayenne pepper has also played a significant role in traditional medicine systems. Long before humans ever stepped into a pharmaceutical laboratory, ancient healers captured the spice's power to heal various health conditions. Today, scientific research provides a microscopic lens to magnify what those that came before knew as fact. Ranging from pain relief and digestion support to cardiovascular health and metabolism enhancement, there was no denying the health benefits of this spicy spice.

In this book, you and I will embark on a journey through the captivating history and the multitude of benefits offered by cayenne pepper. First, we travel back into its origins and early uses, using the map as our guide, tracing its path as it spread across continents and influenced diverse cultures. From there, we explore the pepper's rich culinary heritage to its recipes that elevate its ability to transform dishes to higher heights of deliciousness. Finally, we will investigate the science behind cayenne pepper, revealing the structure of its nutritional composition that is the key to its health-promoting properties. From traditional medicinal uses to modern scientific revelations.

From ancient civilizations to modern times, cayenne pepper has played a crucial role in culinary, medicinal, and cultural contexts. Whether you are a culinary enthusiast seeking to explore new flavors or an individual on a quest for improved health and well-being, I will provide you with a comprehensive understanding of the history, health benefits, and culinary wonders of cayenne pepper. Take a fiery journey with me as we dive into the origins, cultural importance, and medicinal benefits linked with this sensational spice.

As a natural health and wellness researcher, I've provided a few detailed recipes using cayenne pepper for various common ailments. These remedies rely on the potent healing properties of cayenne pepper to address conditions ranging from digestive issues to pain relief. **Always consult with a healthcare provider before using any natural remedy, especially if you have underlying health conditions or are taking medication.**

CHAPTER 1

THE HISTORY

In this chapter, we will explore the origins of cayenne pepper and its early uses. We will uncover its ancient roots within the indigenous cultures of South America. From Mayan rituals to Aztec cuisine, cayenne pepper has left a legacy on civilization.

The story of cayenne pepper begins in the ancient lands of Central and South America, where this fiery spice is known to have its roots. Cultivated in the fertile soils of South America, where its ancestors, known as chilies, grew abundantly. The region's diverse climates and ecosystems provided the perfect conditions for the cultivation and growth of chili peppers. Archaeological findings suggest that chili peppers were first domesticated in what is now Mexico around 6,000 years ago.

Among the early civilizations that embraced the use of cayenne pepper, the Mayans and the Aztecs are widely considered the first early civilizations to embrace the use of cayenne pepper. The Mayans, known for their highly developed agricultural practices, fused chili peppers into their religious rituals. They believed that the spiciness of the peppers embodied the power of the sun and used them in ritualistic offerings to their gods.

The Aztecs, on the other hand, absorbed cayenne pepper into their daily cooking. They not only treasured the spice for its flavor but was conscious of its medicinal properties. Cayenne pepper, also known as chili comes from the Nahutl Aztec language meaning capsicum or peppers. It became a staple ingredient in Aztec daily dishes, enhancing flavors within and added a touch of heat.

In the Inca Empire, there was also a solid connection with this spice. Known as "ucho" or "aji," cayenne pepper played an important role in Inca foods, providing an enjoyable heat to their dishes. The Inca people grew a variety of chili peppers and used them in traditional meals, creating a distinctive flavor profile that reflected their cultural identity.

Cayenne pepper moved to the "new" world in no time. With the arrival of European conquerors and the so-called "age of exploration", the fiery heat of this spice traveled the world. It is reported that Columbus, in his travels voyaged to this region in 1492, was introduced to chili peppers and took them back to Europe. The spice exploded on the scene and soon spread throughout the kitchens of the continents and becoming a most popular trade commodity.

Cayenne Pepper's journey did not stop in Europe. The pepper became a staple product along the Silk Road and Spice Routes. It continued to make its way across the world through ancient trade routes. Traders saw the value and demand for this spice, and it found its way to Africa, Asia, and the Arab nations. In these places, cayenne pepper transformed local cuisines, complimenting the culinary traditions and introducing new levels of heat. The cultural significance of this pepper is enormous. In many cultures, it symbolizes passion, strength, and vitality. It was used in celebrations, festivals, and rituals, becoming an intrinsic part of the cultural fabric. The spice's energetic red color and powerful heat evoked emotions and added a touch of excitement to culinary creations.

Beyond its culinary applications, cayenne pepper was also valued for its medicinal properties by ancient civilizations. The Mayans, Aztecs, Incas, and everyone else recognized its potential to relieve pain, improve gut health, and enhance circulation. They used it daily as a natural remedy for many ailments, including toothaches, sore throats, and digestive issues.

Conclusion

Cayenne pepper's origins can be traced back to Central and South America, where the earliest civilizations grew and cherished this flaming spice. From Aztec, Inca, and Mayan rituals cuisine, cayenne pepper played an important part in the cultural and culinary practices of their society. With the arrival of European colonizers, the spice was trafficked around the globe, enhancing the cuisines and cultures everywhere. Its lively red color, blazing heat, and medicinal properties made it a valued ingredient amongst cooks, shamans, and healers. Let's journey on, exploring this amazing hot spice's culinary applications and examining the medicinal benefits that have fascinated civilizations since that time.

CHAPTER 2

INTERCONTINENTAL REACH

In this chapter, the spice wave reaches the "new" world. I'll trace the journey of cayenne pepper as it travels across deserts and oceans. I will discuss how it captivated the taste buds of traders and people, eventually reaching the farthest places in Africa and Asia. The stories of spice trade routes will reveal how cayenne pepper became a go-to spice across nations and generations.

Cayenne pepper, with its hotness and flaming red color, has roamed far and wide, capturing the taste buds of people on all continents. From its origins in South America to its universal use in dishes around the globe, cayenne pepper has become a star attraction. In this chapter, you will discover how this unbelievable spice traveled so far and wide making its mark, leaving a lasting impact on culinary traditions and cultural practices.

It has been reported that around the time Christopher Columbus beached his ship on the eastern coast of this land cayenne pepper was a natural part of ancient life. On his voyage in 1492, Columbus was introduced to chili peppers, including cayenne pepper, which of course he brought back to Europe. The spice quickly became popular amongst traders who found another thing people loved and were willing to pay for. Cayenne Pepper joined a variety of amazing spices already flowing through Africa and Asia. The spice trade route began over 4000 years ago. Well before the first European conquer was born. Cumin, Black pepper, Turmeric, Ginger, Cinnamon, Clove and Paprika were already in circulation.

In this part of the world, cayenne pepper quickly became "go-to" spice in Europe. From there it traveled the African spice trade routes. They played an important role in the spread of this pepper across the continents. European conquerors Columbus, DeGama and others brought back various kinds of spicy pepper varieties, including cayenne pepper, from their voyages of plunder and destruction of the "New World'. This flood of spices upgraded the European bland cuisine, adding new levels of tastiness. The European love of the spice began.

It is widely known that African explorers had been traveling to the "New World" for centuries before Columbus and others were even born. As it relates to the Cayenne pepper, the African spice routes became the conduit for this pepper. It facilitated the exchange of goods between continents. As cayenne pepper reached Asia, it blended seamlessly with the rich culinary traditions of the region, resulting in uniquely fabulous dishes. In countries such as India, Thailand, and China, cayenne pepper became an essential ingredient, strengthening the spiciness and depth of flavor in traditional dishes. This marriage of flavors led to the development of iconic dishes such as Indian curries, Thai spicy stir-fries, and Chinese hot and sour soups.

As European countries continue to colonize the African continent, they found cayenne pepper enhancing their food as well.

The spice found a place in the diverse African dishes, adding a fiery kick to popular cuisines. In West Africa, cayenne pepper became a key ingredient in popular dishes like "jollof rice" and various stews, while in North Africa, it played a role in the development of spicy blends like harissa. The spice became intertwined with African culinary traditions, showcasing the spice's adaptability and ability to complement a range of flavors.

Cayenne Pepper also has a Caribbean connection. The spice originated in the South American continent; its journey did not end there. The spice continued to spread within the continent, finding its way into the cuisines throughout the region. In Mexico, cayenne pepper became a staple in dishes like salsa and mole, adding a distinct heat and depth of flavor. In the Caribbean, it along with island favorite Scotch Bonnet pepper, added great value to the development of vibrant spice blends such as jerk seasoning and curry, infusing the region's cuisine with an additional fiery Caribbean twist.

In the modern era of globalization, cayenne pepper has reached every corner of the globe. The ease of transportation and the interconnectivity of cultures have allowed the spice to transcend boundaries and become a staple in diverse cuisines. Today, cayenne pepper can be found in dishes from all continents, from spicy curries in India to fiery hot wings in the United States, from chili-infused chocolates in Europe to piquant soups in Asia. Its versatility and ability to adapt to different culinary traditions have made it a cherished ingredient worldwide.

Conclusion

Cayenne pepper's journey from the South American continent to the rest of the globe is a testament to its universal appeal. The spice's introduction to Europe set in motion a culinary revolution, and its subsequent spread through spice trade routes and cultural exchange left an indelible mark on cuisines across continents. Today, cayenne pepper continues to be celebrated and embraced as a spice that adds heat, depth, and excitement to dishes worldwide. Its journey highlights the power of spices to bridge cultures, enrich culinary traditions, and ignite the taste buds of people from diverse backgrounds.

CHAPTER 3

CULINARY AND MEDICINAL USES

Cayenne pepper is not just a spice that adds heat and upgrades the flavor of dishes worldwide; it has a rich history of culinary and medicinal applications. In this chapter, we will explore the diverse uses of cayenne pepper in the culinary world, where it is celebrated for its ability to enhance flavors and create unique culinary dishes. Additionally, we will dive a little deeper into its historical medicinal uses, where it has been employed for many centuries to address various health concerns. If you have a copy of my book "Unlocking the Power of Castor Oil: Your Guide to Natural Beauty and Well-Being" you will find DIY recipes using Castor oil and Cayenne pepper. From tantalizing taste buds to promoting well-being, cayenne pepper offers a world of possibilities in both the kitchen and the medicine cabinet.

Medicinal Applications

Cayenne pepper has long been revered for its beneficial effects on digestive health. The spice stimulates saliva production and gastric juices, aiding in digestion. It has been used to alleviate digestive discomfort, relieve gas and bloating, and promote a healthy metabolism. Additionally, cayenne pepper's warming properties have been suggested to help soothe stomach ulcers.

Pain Relief Cayenne pepper contains a compound called capsaicin, which is known for its pain-relieving properties. When applied topically with a carrier oil such as Castor oil, capsaicin desensitizes pain receptors and provides relief from various types of chronic pain, such as arthritis, muscle aches, and nerve pain. It is commonly found in topical creams and patches used for pain management.

Research and personal testimonies indicate that cayenne pepper may have positive effects on cardiovascular health. It has been found to promote healthy blood circulation by helping to lower blood pressure, reduce inflammation and reduce the risk of blood clot formation. As the spice travels the bloodstream, it repairs any micro tares it finds. Additionally, cayenne pepper's warming properties may improve blood flow and promote the overall health of blood vessels.

Respiratory Health Cayenne pepper's heat and spice can help promote respiratory health. It acts as a natural decongestant, helping to clear congestion and relieve symptoms of respiratory conditions like sinusitis, allergies, and common colds. Combining the use of this spice with the massage techniques shared in the book "Facial Fitness: Revolutionize Your Self-care with Facial Exercises and Holistic Massage Techniques for Neck and Decolletage" will maximize your respiratory and sinus relief. Cayenne pepper's ability to stimulate mucus flow and open up nasal passages can provide relief from congestion and improve breathing.

Capsaicin, the active compound in cayenne pepper, has been studied for its potential to support weight management. It has been found to increase metabolism and enhance the fat-burning process. Incorporating cayenne pepper into a balanced diet and active lifestyle may help boost calorie expenditure and promote weight loss. Adding a little heat to tropical oils like organic castor oil used to target belly fat would help promote fat burning.

Conclusion

Cayenne pepper offers a diverse range of culinary and medicinal applications. From adding fiery heat and enhancing flavors in various dishes to supporting digestive health, respiratory health, reduction of inflammation and providing pain relief, this versatile spice has been valued by ancient cultures well before there was an America or Europe. Whether it's spicing up your favorite recipes or harnessing its medicinal properties, cayenne pepper continues to captivate and benefit individuals in both the culinary and medicinal realms. Its wide array of applications makes it a staple in kitchens and medicine cabinets around the world.

CHAPTER 4

NUTRITIONAL VALUE AND HEALTH BENEFITS OF CAYENNE PEPPER

Beyond its taste and culinary applications, cayenne pepper offers an impressive array of nutritional value and health benefits. This chapter will explore the composition of cayenne pepper, highlighting its rich nutrient content and the positive impact it can have on human health. From vitamins and minerals to antioxidant and anti-inflammatory properties, cayenne pepper proves to be a powerful ally in promoting overall well-being.

Cayenne pepper, a nutrient-dense spice, is a nutritional powerhouse, packing a range of essential vitamins, minerals, and beneficial plant compounds. While the exact nutritional profile may vary depending on the variety and preparation of the spice, the Cayenne pepper is an excellent source of various vitamins.

It is particularly high in vitamin C, an essential nutrient that supports the immune system, aids in collagen production, and acts as an antioxidant. In fact, a single teaspoon of cayenne pepper can provide a significant portion of the recommended daily intake of vitamin C.

Furthermore, cayenne pepper contains vitamin A, which is crucial for maintaining healthy vision, promoting cell growth, and supporting immune function. It also contains small amounts of vitamins E and K, which play important roles in maintaining healthy skin, cardiovascular health, and bone health.

Cayenne pepper is a good source of minerals that are vital for various bodily functions. It contains significant amounts of potassium, an essential electrolyte that helps regulate fluid balance, nerve function, and muscle contractions. Additionally, cayenne pepper provides small amounts of manganese, magnesium, and iron, which are necessary for energy production, bone health, and oxygen transport in the body.

Cayenne pepper contains a compound called capsaicin, which is responsible for its spicy taste and also contributes to its health benefits. Capsaicin is a potent antioxidant and anti-inflammatory agent. Antioxidants help protect cells from damage caused by free radicals and unstable molecules that can contribute to various diseases and the aging process. By neutralizing free radicals, the antioxidants in cayenne pepper can help reduce the risk of chronic diseases, such as heart disease, cancer, and neurodegenerative disorders.

Additionally, capsaicin has been shown to possess anti-inflammatory properties. It is widely known that where there is pain there is also inflammation. However, chronic inflammation is linked to the development of many diseases, including heart disease, diabetes, and arthritis. The anti-inflammatory effects of cayenne pepper will help alleviate inflammation and reduce the risk of these conditions and more.

Cayenne pepper has gained attention for its potential to boost metabolism and support weight management. Capsaicin, the active compound in cayenne pepper, has been found to increase thermogenesis, which is the process by which the body generates heat and burns calories. By raising the body's core temperature, capsaicin can help increase calorie expenditure and promote weight loss. In addition, cayenne pepper may aid in appetite control and reduce calorie intake. It has been found to suppress appetite and increase feelings of fullness, which can contribute to reduced calorie consumption and ultimately support weight management efforts.

Cardiovascular Health Studies have suggested that cayenne pepper may have beneficial effects on cardiovascular health. Capsaicin has been found to promote healthy blood circulation by dilating blood vessels and improving blood flow. It may also help lower blood pressure levels, reduce LDL (bad) cholesterol, and prevent the formation of blood clots, thus reducing the risk of heart disease and stroke. I half teaspoon of medicinal cayenne pepper taken by mouth can save someone's life.

The capsaicin in cayenne pepper has been recognized for its potential to provide pain relief. When applied topically, capsaicin can desensitize pain receptors, leading to temporary relief from various types of pain, including arthritis, neuropathy, and muscle soreness. Topical creams and ointments containing capsaicin are commonly used as natural remedies for pain management.

Conclusion

Cayenne pepper offers more than just a fiery taste—it is a nutritional powerhouse with a range of health benefits. Its rich nutrient content, antioxidant and anti-inflammatory properties, metabolism-boosting effects, and potential for cardiovascular health and pain relief make it a valuable daily addition to a healthy diet and lifestyle. Incorporating cayenne pepper into your meals and utilizing its medicinal properties can contribute to overall well-being and enhance your journey to DOMINATE your days.

**If you are taking a blood thinner do not consume large amounts of cayenne pepper. Consult your physician!

CHAPTER 5

TRADITIONAL MEDICINE

Cayenne pepper's fiery reputation extends beyond its culinary applications. Historically, the ancestors have used this versatile spice in reverence for its medicinal properties. Since the time of the ancients, cayenne pepper played a significant role in traditional medicine systems as it spread around the world. We will highlight its role in Ayurveda in healing practices. We will also dive a little deeper into the historical use of cayenne pepper in traditional medicine, into the belief systems, and various applications of this amazing spice in promoting well-being and addressing specific health concerns. From ancient civilizations and indigenous cultures, cayenne pepper has been utilized to address a wide range of health concerns and promote overall well-being.

Indigenous cultures worldwide have recognized the healing potential of cayenne pepper and have incorporated it into their traditional healing practices. For instance, Native American tribes have used cayenne pepper to alleviate pain, soothe digestive discomfort, and enhance circulation. The plant's medicinal properties were also valued by the indigenous peoples of the lands now known as the Americas, who employed it to address a range of health concerns, including sore throats, toothaches, and digestive issues.

In the ancient Indian system of Ayurveda, cayenne pepper, known as "Lal Mirch" or "Maricha," is prominent. According to Ayurvedic principles, cayenne pepper is believed to possess heating properties, known as "ushna virya," which can stimulate digestion, improve circulation, and promote detoxification. It is often used in Ayurvedic formulations to support healthy digestion, enhance metabolism, and alleviate respiratory congestion.

To the Chinese, the Cayenne pepper, referred to as "Chao Tian Jiao" in Traditional Chinese Medicine, is valued for its ability to invigorate blood circulation and dispel coldness from the body. In this culture, it is often used to warm the body, alleviate pain, and improve digestion. Cayenne pepper is also believed to have a positive effect on the spleen and stomach meridians, promoting overall well-being and restoring balance in the body.

This fiery pepper has long been utilized as a digestive aid and stimulant. Its active compound, capsaicin, is believed to stimulate saliva production, increase gastric juices, and improve digestion. It is thought to enhance the metabolism of fats and proteins, promote nutrient absorption, and alleviate digestive discomfort, such as indigestion and bloating.

Cayenne pepper's warming properties have led to its inclusion in traditional detoxification practices. It is believed and research now shows, that the spice stimulates circulation, increase sweating, and promote the elimination of toxins from the body. This aspect of cayenne pepper's traditional use aligns with its potential as a diaphoretic, a substance that induces perspiration and assists the body in eliminating waste products. Marry this spice with a lymphatic drainage routine and detoxify your body daily.

Traditional medicinal systems often recognize cayenne pepper's potential to support circulatory health. It is believed to improve blood flow, dilate blood vessels, and promote healthy cardiovascular function. By enhancing blood circulation, cayenne pepper contributes to optimal organ function and overall vitality.

Applied topically, cayenne pepper's active component, capsaicin, is well-known for its analgesic properties. When applied topically, capsaicin can desensitize nerve endings, providing temporary pain relief. Traditional medicine practitioners have used cayenne pepper preparations externally to alleviate muscle and joint pain, arthritis, and nerve-related discomfort.

Cayenne pepper has a long-standing tradition of use in addressing respiratory congestion. It is believed to have expectorant properties, promoting the expulsion of mucus and clearing nasal passages. Traditional remedies often combine cayenne pepper with other ingredients to create nasal sprays, chest rubs, or herbal teas that can provide relief from congestion due to allergies, colds, or respiratory infections.

The warming nature of cayenne pepper has led to its association with immune-stimulating properties. Traditional medicine systems suggest that cayenne pepper can help fortify the body's defenses and promote overall immune health. It is often used as an ingredient in remedies aimed at boosting immune function and reducing susceptibility to infections due to its antimicrobial properties.

Conclusion

Cayenne pepper has held a significant place in traditional medicine systems throughout history. From indigenous healing practices to Chinese and Indian medicine, it has been utilized for its digestive, circulatory, pain-relieving, and respiratory benefits. While modern scientific research continues to explore the mechanisms behind these traditional uses, the rich historical legacy of cayenne pepper in traditional medicine serves as a testament to its enduring reputation as a valuable medicinal spice.

Keep It Spicy: Be a Hero with Your Review

"The best way to find yourself is to lose yourself in the service of others." – Mahatma Gandhi

Guess what? People who do kind things for others without waiting for a "*thank you*" often feel happier and more fulfilled. Imagine if we could spread that kind of happiness around! Now, I've got something important to ask you... *Would you be willing to do a small, good deed for someone you've never met?* Even if no one else knew you did it?

Think about it. This person is a lot like you, or maybe like you were once upon a time. They're eager to learn, wanting to make a positive change in their life, and searching for the right guidance but not sure where to turn.

My dream is to make *Cayenne Pepper: The History. The Heat. The Health.* a tool for everyone. My whole heart is in this mission. To reach this dream, I need to connect with... everyone. And this is where you, my dear reader, come into play. H*ere's my heartfelt request on behalf of those actively seeking natural remedies for health and beauty who haven't met you yet:*

Please consider leaving a review for this book.

It won't cost you a dime, only a minute of your time, but it could make a world of difference for another person looking to enhance their health. Your review might be the key to...

… supporting more small businesses in our communities. ...helping another woman provide for her family. ...empowering someone to find meaningful work. ...assisting another in transforming their life. ...making another person's dream a reality.

Feeling that warm, fuzzy feeling inside? That's the joy of helping. And it's super easy to do - just takes a moment to leave a review.

Simply share your thoughts on the website (Amazon, BarnesandNoble, etc.) where you purchased this book.

If you're excited about making a positive impact on someone's journey toward natural and gentle beauty care, then you're exactly who I'm looking for. **Welcome to the family!**

I can't wait to read your review and hear how this book has helped you to boost your health, eliminate digestive problems, and find relief from pain. A huge thank you from the bottom of my heart. Let's get back to discovering more about cayenne pepper together.

Your biggest cheerleader, Dr. Andrea Blake-Garrett

P.S. - Here's a little secret: when you share something valuable, you become even more valued. **If you know another who would benefit from this book, why not spread the love?**

CHAPTER 6

THE HEAT – CULINARY APPLICATIONS

Cayenne pepper's culinary applications are vast and varied, making it a beloved spice in kitchens around the world. In this chapter, we will explore the numerous ways in which cayenne pepper, as a key ingredient, can enhance culinary creations, from appetizers and main courses, beverages, sauces and desserts. Its fiery heat, vibrant color, and distinct flavor profile contribute to a wide range of culinary delights that are sure to please the palate and ignite the taste buds.

One of the primary culinary uses of cayenne pepper is as a flavor enhancer. Its fiery heat and distinct flavor profile make it a popular choice in a wide range of dishes. Whether it's sprinkled on eggs, added to soups and stews, used to season meats and vegetables or blended into a spicy drink, cayenne pepper provides a spicy kick that elevates the overall taste and experience of everything.

The making of a variety of culinary spice blends and sauccs includes Cayenne pepper. It is an key component in spice blends like curry powder, chili powder, and Cajun seasoning. These blends are used to add depth and complexity to dishes, showcasing the spice's ability to complement and enhance other flavors. Similarly, cayenne pepper plays a prominent role in hot sauces, salsas, and marinades, providing a fiery heat and enhancing the overall flavor profile.

Cayenne pepper is often used in pickling and fermentation processes. Its heat helps to preserve and add flavor to vegetables, fruits, and even meats. The spice's antimicrobial properties contribute to the preservation of pickled foods and aid in the fermentation process, allowing for the development of unique and tangy flavors.

While cayenne pepper is commonly associated with savory dishes, it can also be found in unexpected places—baked goods and desserts. The spice adds a subtle heat and depth to chocolate-based desserts like brownies, truffles, and cakes. The combination of the spice's warmth and the sweetness of the dessert creates a delightful contrast that tantalizes the taste buds.

Cayenne pepper's fiery heat and distinct flavor make it a perfect ingredient for spice blends, sauces and condiments. Whether it's a classic hot sauce, a tangy barbecue sauce, or a zesty salsa, cayenne pepper adds a punch of heat that elevates the flavor profile of these condiments. The spice's versatility allows for endless variations, from mild and tangy to bold and blazing.

Cayenne pepper is a go-to spice for marinades and rubs, infusing meats, poultry, and even vegetables with its distinct heat and flavor. When combined with other herbs and spices to make "Dry Jerk seasoning, curry, etc., cayenne pepper adds depth and complexity to marinades, enhancing the taste and tenderness of grilled or roasted dishes. Its vibrant red color creates an appetizing visual appeal as well.

Cayenne pepper plays a vital role in a variety of seasonings and spice blends. It is a key ingredient in popular blends like Cajun seasoning, curry powder, and chili powder, adding a kick of heat and a depth of flavor to these mixtures. Sprinkling cayenne pepper into everyday seasonings can instantly transform a dish, imparting a spicy and aromatic element.

Dishes cayenne pepper is a staple in many Asian cuisines, where it is celebrated for its ability to add a fiery kick to dishes. In Thai cuisine, cayenne pepper is a key ingredient in stir-fries, curries, and noodle dishes, providing a balance of heat and flavor. Similarly, in Indian cuisine, it is a vital component of spice blends, such as garam masala, and is used to create spicy curries and chutneys.

Cayenne pepper's influence is particularly prominent in Latin American cuisine, where it is an essential spice in dishes from Mexico to the Caribbean. In Mexican cuisine, it brings heat and complexity to salsas, enchiladas, and mole sauces. In the Caribbean, it is a cornerstone of jerk seasoning, imparting a fiery and aromatic flavor to grilled meats and seafood.

Cayenne pepper's versatility allows it to be embraced in global fusion dishes that bring together diverse culinary traditions. It can be used to add a spicy twist to Italian pasta sauces, Spanish paellas, Moroccan tagines, and more. The spice's ability to complement and enhance flavors from various regions makes it a valuable ingredient for creative chefs and home cooks alike.

The combination of cayenne pepper's heat and chocolate's richness creates a tantalizing flavor experience. In desserts like spicy chocolate truffles, brownies, and hot chocolate, cayenne pepper adds a subtle, warming kick that balances the sweetness and adds a layer of complexity. The contrasting flavors make for an unforgettable culinary adventure.

Cayenne pepper can be used to create fruit-infused syrups, sauces, and treats that add a spicy twist to sweet treats. Infusing fruits like mangoes, strawberries, or pineapples with cayenne pepper creates a delightful blend of sweetness and heat. Slices of fresh ripe mangoes sprinkled with cayenne pepper and other select spices are a "must have". These spicy fruit syrups can be drizzled over pancakes, waffles, ice-cream, or incorporated into cocktails for a unique flavor experience.

For those seeking a culinary thrill while enjoying baked goods, cayenne pepper can be incorporated into recipes like spiced cookies, cakes, and bread. Its addition can create an unexpected burst of heat that complements the sweetness of the baked goods. From cinnamon-cayenne snickerdoodles to chocolate-cayenne cupcakes and cookies, these creations are sure to excite and delight the taste buds.

Conclusion

Cayenne pepper's culinary applications are indeed vast and varied, offering a world of possibilities in the kitchen. Whether adding fiery heat to sauces and condiments, infusing international cuisines with a spicy kick, or creating unexpected flavor combinations in desserts and sweet treats, cayenne pepper elevates the culinary experience. Its ability to balance flavors, enhance dishes, and ignite the taste buds make it an essential spice for those seeking culinary delights that go beyond the ordinary.

Cayenne Pepper Immune-Boosting Soup

This immune-boosting soup is packed with nutrients and the heat of cayenne pepper can help stimulate the immune system, making it perfect during cold and flu season.

Ingredients:

- 1/4 teaspoon of cayenne pepper powder
- 1 onion, chopped
- 3 cloves garlic, minced
- 1 tablespoon of olive oil
- 4 cups of vegetable broth
- 1 cup of chopped carrots
- 1 cup of chopped celery
- 1 cup of chopped kale or collard greens
- Juice of 1 lemon

Instructions:

1. In a large pot, heat olive oil over medium heat.
2. Add onion and garlic, sauté until softened.
3. Add carrots and celery, cook for another 5 minutes.
4. Pour in the vegetable broth and bring to a boil.
5. Reduce heat and simmer for 20 minutes.

6. Stir in the cayenne pepper, kale/collard greens, and lemon juice.

7. Simmer for an additional 5 minutes.

8. Serve hot.

Cayenne Pepper Detox Drink

This detox drink can help cleanse the digestive system, boost metabolism, and support weight loss efforts.

Ingredients:

- 1/4 teaspoon of cayenne pepper powder
- 2 tablespoons of lemon juice
- 1 tablespoon of Organic raw honey
- 1 cup of water

Instructions:

1. Combine all ingredients in a glass of water.

2. Stir well and drink in the morning on an empty stomach.

3. Repeat daily for up to two weeks.

CHAPTER 7

MODERN SCIENCE – THE HEALTH

The modern scientific community has taken a deliberate interest in cayenne pepper, conducting numerous studies to uncover its secrets. In this chapter, we will look at the latest scientific discoveries regarding the spice, shedding light on its potential health benefits and the mechanisms behind its effects. From its impact on pain management to its role as a cardiovascular health enhancer, natural pain reliever, and metabolism booster, these scientific findings provide a deeper understanding of the remarkable properties of cayenne pepper.

One of the most extensively studied aspects of cayenne pepper is its active compound, capsaicin, and its impact on pain relief and management. Capsaicin has been found to desensitize pain receptors by depleting substance P, a neurotransmitter involved in transmitting pain signals. When applied topically, capsaicin can desensitize pain receptors, leading to temporary relief from conditions such as arthritis, musculoskeletal pain, and neuropathy.

Capsaicin-based topical creams and ointments have been extensively researched for their analgesic effects. They are available in pharmacies near you, or you can make your own. When applied to the skin, capsaicin stimulates the release of endorphins, natural pain-relieving compounds in the body. This mechanism helps provide temporary relief from localized pain and has been used successfully in the management of conditions like osteoarthritis.

Research suggests that cayenne pepper's active compound, capsaicin, promotes vasodilation—the widening of blood vessels—resulting in improved blood flow and lowered blood pressure. Capsaicin activates receptors in the blood vessel walls, triggering the release of nitric oxide, a molecule that relaxes and dilates blood vessels. This vasodilatory effect contributes to cardiovascular health and may reduce the risk of hypertension and related conditions.

Blood Clot Prevention Studies have shown that capsaicin may possess antiplatelet and anticoagulant properties, which help prevent the formation of blood clots. It inhibits the aggregation of platelets, preventing them from clumping together and forming clots that can lead to heart attacks or strokes. This finding suggests that cayenne pepper's active components may have a protective effect on the cardiovascular system. By maintaining healthy blood flow and preventing clotting, cayenne pepper may contribute to a healthier cardiovascular system. Avoid this spice if you are taking blood thinning medications.

Capsaicin has been found to increase thermogenesis, the process by which the body generates heat and burns calories. It stimulates the activation of brown adipose fat tissue, which is responsible for generating heat and burning stored fat. This thermogenic effect can lead to increased caloric expenditure, making cayenne pepper a potential ally in weight management efforts.

Intake Research suggests that capsaicin can help reduce appetite and promote satiety, thereby decreasing overall caloric intake. It activates the TRPV1 receptor in the gastrointestinal tract, triggering the release of hormones that signal fullness. By curbing hunger and reducing the desire to eat, cayenne pepper may support weight loss and weight maintenance.

Cayenne pepper contains various antioxidants, including vitamins C and E, which help neutralize harmful free radicals and reduce oxidative stress in the body. Antioxidants help protect cells from damage and play a crucial role in reducing the risk of chronic diseases such as heart disease, cancer, and neurodegenerative disorders.

Inflammation is a common underlying factor in various chronic conditions, such as arthritis and inflammatory bowel disease. Capsaicin's anti-inflammatory properties have been the focus of several studies. It has been found to inhibit the production of inflammatory compounds and reduce the activity of pro-inflammatory enzymes mitigating the inflammatory response and providing relief. This anti-inflammatory action suggests that cayenne pepper has potential pain relief benefits for individuals with conditions characterized by chronic inflammation, such as arthritis and certain digestive disorders.

Emerging research suggests that capsaicin may have anticancer properties. Studies have shown that capsaicin can induce cell death (apoptosis) and inhibit the growth and spread of cancer cells in various types of cancer, including prostate, colorectal, and breast cancers.

These findings highlight the potential for cayenne pepper as a natural compound in cancer prevention and treatment.

Conclusion

Modern scientific research has revealed exciting discoveries regarding the health benefits of cayenne pepper. From its role in pain management and cardiovascular health to its effects on metabolism, weight management and cancer, cayenne pepper's active compound, capsaicin, has been the subject of extensive investigation. The findings underscore its potential as a natural remedy for various conditions, while also shedding light on the mechanisms underlying its effects. As research continues to uncover the secrets of cayenne pepper, its medicinal properties are being validated, further highlighting its importance as a spice that offers more than just a fiery flavor.

CHAPTER 8

OTHER USES AND SURPRISING FACTS

Beyond the kitchen and the medicine cabinet, cayenne pepper has found unexpected applications. In this chapter, we will explore the diverse uses of cayenne pepper beyond its culinary and medicinal purposes. From gardening and pest control to personal care and self-defense, cayenne pepper reveals its versatility in various domains. Additionally, we will uncover some surprising facts about this spice that highlight its unique characteristics and historical significance.

In The Garden

In gardening, cayenne pepper can serve as a soil amendment to enhance plant growth. The spice contains beneficial nutrients like nitrogen, phosphorus, and potassium, which are essential for plant health. Mixing cayenne pepper into the soil can enrich its nutrient content and improve soil structure, promoting the growth of healthy and robust plants.

Cayenne pepper can be used as a natural pesticide to deter pests from damaging plants. When sprinkled around plants or mixed with water to create a spray, cayenne pepper acts as a deterrent for pests like aphids, caterpillars, and slugs. Its pungent aroma and spicy taste make plants less appealing to these unwanted visitors, protecting your growing garden without the use of Toxic chemicals getting into the food you will eat.

Personal Care and Beauty

Cayenne Pepper and Castor Oil Hair Growth Serum

Cayenne pepper has been used in hair care products to promote hair growth and improve scalp health. Its stimulating properties help increase blood flow to the scalp, which can aid in hair follicle health and promote hair growth. Additionally, cayenne pepper's natural antifungal properties may help address scalp issues such as dandruff and fungal infections. Again, a blend of Organic Cold Pressed Hexane Free Castor oil and cayenne pepper will add great value to you scalp and hair.

A blend of organic cold-pressed hexane-free castor oil and cayenne pepper can create a potent hair growth serum. The capsaicin in cayenne pepper stimulates blood flow to the scalp, promoting healthy hair follicles, while castor oil nourishes and strengthens the hair shaft. To use, apply a small amount of the serum to the scalp, massage gently, and leave it on for a few hours or overnight before washing it out.

Ingredients:

- 3 tablespoons of castor oil
- 1 teaspoon of cayenne pepper powder

Cayenne Pepper Infused Hair Oil

Infusing hair oil with cayenne pepper can help boost scalp circulation and combat hair thinning. Olive oil or coconut oil can be used as a base, providing additional moisture and nourishment to the hair. The infusion process involves steeping cayenne pepper in the chosen oil for a few days to a week, then straining out the solids.

Ingredients:

- 1 cup of olive oil or coconut oil
- 1 teaspoons of cayenne pepper flakes

Cayenne Pepper and Aloe Vera Scalp Treatment

Combining cayenne pepper with soothing aloe vera gel creates a balanced scalp treatment that stimulates hair growth while calming any irritation. Aloe vera's hydrating and anti-inflammatory properties complement the stimulating effects of cayenne pepper, making it suitable for sensitive scalps.

Ingredients:

- 1/2 cup of aloe vera gel
- 1/2 teaspoon of cayenne pepper powder

Cayenne Pepper Hair Mask

A hair mask that includes cayenne pepper, honey, and yogurt can provide deep conditioning and stimulation to the scalp. Honey is a natural humectant that locks in moisture, while yogurt adds protein and probiotics that nourish the hair. For best results, this mask can be applied once a week.

Ingredients:

- 2 tablespoons of yogurt
- 1 tablespoon of honey
- 1/2 teaspoon of cayenne pepper powder

Cayenne Pepper and Essential Oil Scalp Massage Oil

A scalp massage oil that blends cayenne pepper with essential oils such as rosemary and peppermint can invigorate the scalp and promote hair growth. Rosemary oil is known for its ability to improve circulation and stimulate hair follicles, while peppermint oil provides a refreshing, cooling sensation.

Ingredients:

- 1/4 cup of jojoba oil or almond oil
- 10 drops of rosemary essential oil
- 10 drops of peppermint essential oil
- 1/2 teaspoon of cayenne pepper powder

How to Use These Products:

1. **Application**: For oils and serums, apply directly to the scalp, massaging gently to ensure even distribution and stimulation of blood flow.

2. **Leave-in Time**: Depending on the product and spice tolerance, leave it on for 30 minutes to a few hours. Some products, like the hair growth serum, can be left on overnight.

3. **Rinsing**: Rinse thoroughly with lukewarm water and follow up with a gentle shampoo to remove any residue. Rinse with head tilted back. Avoid pepper getting in your eyes, ears and nasal passages.

4. **Frequency**: Use these treatments 1-2 times per week for best results, adjusting the frequency based on individual hair and scalp needs.

By incorporating cayenne pepper into these hair care products, you can leverage its natural properties to promote healthy hair growth and improve scalp health.

Skincare

The warming and invigorating properties of cayenne pepper have led to its inclusion in skincare products. When used topically, it can increase blood circulation and provide a natural glow to the skin. Some formulations may incorporate cayenne pepper to address skin concerns like acne, as its antibacterial properties can help reduce inflammation and promote clearer skin.

By incorporating cayenne pepper into these skincare products, you can take advantage of its natural properties to enhance blood circulation, reduce inflammation, and promote a healthy, radiant complexion.

Cayenne Pepper Facial Mask

A facial mask that includes cayenne pepper, honey, and yogurt can provide a deep-cleansing and revitalizing treatment for the skin. The capsaicin in cayenne pepper stimulates blood flow, honey acts as a natural humectant with antibacterial properties, and yogurt soothes and moisturizes the skin.

Ingredients:

- 2 tablespoons of plain yogurt
- 1 tablespoon of honey
- 1/4 teaspoon of cayenne pepper powder

Application: Mix the ingredients to form a paste, apply evenly to the face, and leave on for 10-15 minutes before rinsing off with lukewarm water.

Cayenne Pepper Body Scrub

A body scrub featuring cayenne pepper, sugar, and coconut oil can exfoliate the skin, improve circulation, and leave the skin feeling smooth and invigorated. The sugar provides gentle exfoliation, while coconut oil hydrates and nourishes the skin.

Ingredients:

- 1 cup of sugar
- 1/2 cup of coconut oil (melted)
- 1 teaspoon of cayenne pepper powder

Application: Combine the ingredients, gently massage onto damp skin in circular motions, and rinse thoroughly with warm water. Take care oil will clog your shower drain.

Cayenne Pepper and Turmeric Face Cleanser

A facial cleanser that combines cayenne pepper with turmeric and aloe vera gel can help reduce inflammation and promote clearer skin. Turmeric's anti-inflammatory properties complement the stimulating effects of cayenne pepper, while aloe vera soothes the skin.

Ingredients:

- 1/4 cup of aloe vera gel
- 1/4 teaspoon of cayenne pepper powder
- 1/4 teaspoon of turmeric powder

Application: Mix the ingredients, apply to the face using gentle circular motions, and rinse with lukewarm water.

Cayenne Pepper Lip Plumper Balm

A lip balm infused with cayenne pepper can create a natural plumping effect by increasing blood flow to the lips. Combined with nourishing oils, this balm can keep lips hydrated and fuller-looking.

Ingredients:

- 1 tablespoon of beeswax pellets
- 1 tablespoon of coconut oil
- 1 tablespoon of shea butter
- 1/4 teaspoon of cayenne pepper powder

Application: Melt the beeswax, coconut oil, and shea butter together, stir in the cayenne pepper, pour into a small container, and let it cool before applying to the lips.

Cayenne Pepper and Green Tea Toner

A toner made with cayenne pepper and green tea can invigorate the skin and provide antioxidant benefits. Green tea is rich in antioxidants, and the addition of cayenne pepper stimulates blood flow, enhancing the skin's natural glow.

Ingredients:

- 1 cup of brewed green tea (cooled)
- 1/8 teaspoon of cayenne pepper powder

Application: Combine the ingredients, pour into a spray bottle, and spritz onto the face after cleansing. Alternatively, apply with a cotton pad.

How to Use These Products:

1. **Patch Test**: Before using any cayenne pepper-based skincare product, perform a patch test on a small area of skin to ensure there is no adverse reaction.
2. **Application**: Follow the recommended application methods for each product, ensuring even and gentle application.
3. **Rinsing**: Thoroughly rinse off products like masks, scrubs, and cleansers with lukewarm water.
4. **Moisturizing**: After using these products, follow up with a moisturizer to keep the skin hydrated and supple.
5. **Frequency**: Use these treatments 1-2 times per week, adjusting the frequency based on individual skin needs and sensitivity.

Pepper Spray

Cayenne pepper's potent heat and capsaicin content make it an effective ingredient in homemade pepper sprays. When combined with a liquid carrier like water or oil, cayenne pepper can be used as a self-defense tool. The spray irritates the eyes and respiratory system, causing temporary discomfort and allowing individuals to escape potentially dangerous situations.

Animal Repellent

Cayenne pepper can be used as a natural deterrent to keep animals away from gardens, trash cans, or other areas where they are not wanted. The strong aroma and spicy taste of cayenne pepper are effective in repelling animals like squirrels, rabbits, and deer, helping to protect plants and property without causing harm to the animals.

Surprising Facts

1. The heat of cayenne pepper is often measured using the Scoville scale, a measurement system developed by pharmacist Wilbur Scoville in 1912. Cayenne pepper typically ranges between 30,000 to 50,000 Scoville Heat Units (SHU), indicating its spiciness. However, some varieties can reach even higher levels of heat, making it one of the hotter peppers in the world.

2. Cayenne pepper holds cultural and culinary symbolism in many regions. In some cultures, it is associated with passion, energy, and vigor. It is believed to ignite the fire within and bring vitality to dishes. The vibrant red color of cayenne pepper also adds visual appeal to culinary creations, making it a popular choice for enhancing presentation.

3. Cayenne pepper's culinary versatility is worth mentioning once again. Its heat and flavor make it a staple in cuisines worldwide, from spicy dishes to milder recipes that simply

require a touch of warmth. Its ability to complement and enhance a wide range of flavors and ingredients makes it an indispensable spice in the kitchen.

Conclusion

Cayenne pepper's uses extend beyond the kitchen and the medicine cabinet. Whether in gardening and pest control, personal care and beauty, or self-defense and personal safety, cayenne pepper showcases its versatility in various aspects of life. Its surprising applications and historical significance add to its allure, making it a spice that offers more than just culinary and medicinal benefits. From repelling pests to promoting hair growth, cayenne pepper continues to surprise and inspire with its wide range of uses.

CHAPTER 9

Conclusion

In this final chapter, let's reflect on the journey we have taken through the history, benefits, and versatile applications of cayenne pepper. We have explored its culinary, medicinal, and surprising uses, unveiling its remarkable properties and the impact it can have on our lives. As we look to the future, it is clear that cayenne pepper's fiery potential continues to ignite interest and open new possibilities.

Health and Well-being

Cayenne pepper's rich nutritional content, antioxidant properties, and potential health benefits make it a valuable addition to a balanced and healthy lifestyle. Traditional wisdom and modern scientific research support its role in pain management, cardiovascular health, metabolism, and digestion. For readers seeking natural remedies and ways to optimize their well-being, cayenne pepper provides an enticing avenue for exploration.

Culinary Innovation and Global Fusion

The culinary world constantly evolves, and cayenne pepper remains a dynamic and indispensable spice. Its fiery heat, vibrant color, and distinct flavor profile add depth and complexity to a wide range of dishes. As chefs and home cooks continue to experiment with global flavors and fusion cuisine, cayenne pepper's versatility allows it to play a starring role in creative culinary endeavors. Its ability to complement diverse ingredients and enhance flavors positions it as a spice that will continue to inspire culinary innovation.

Sustainable Agriculture and Environmental Impact

As our society becomes increasingly conscious of the environmental impact of our choices, cayenne pepper offers a potential solution. Its cultivation and production can align with the principles of sustainable agriculture. Organic farming practices can minimize pesticide use, reduce water consumption, and promote biodiversity. By supporting sustainable farming methods and purchasing cayenne pepper from responsible sources, we can contribute to a more environmentally friendly future.

Cultural Appreciation and Culinary Heritage

Cayenne pepper's significance goes beyond its taste and medicinal properties. It holds cultural and historical importance in various regions, and its inclusion in traditional cuisines reflects centuries of culinary heritage. By appreciating and embracing the cultural origins of cayenne pepper, we can celebrate the diversity of flavors and traditions that enrich our culinary experiences.

Continued Exploration and Research

While we have uncovered many aspects of cayenne pepper's history, benefits, and applications, there is still much to discover. As the scientific research continues to explore its properties and potential, new findings may emerge, deepening our understanding of its effects on human health and opening doors to further applications. The journey of cayenne pepper is an ongoing one, filled with possibilities and opportunities for continued exploration.

Modern scientific research has shed light on the myriad health benefits associated with cayenne pepper. Its active compound, capsaicin, has been extensively studied for its pain-relieving, anti-inflammatory, and metabolism-boosting properties. Research indicates that cayenne pepper may play a role in promoting cardiovascular health, supporting weight management, and even offering potential anticancer effects.

The future of cayenne pepper in health and wellness looks promising as scientists continue to uncover new therapeutic uses. The development of capsaicin-based pharmaceuticals and supplements is an area of growing interest, potentially offering natural and effective treatments for a range of health conditions. Additionally, the integration of cayenne pepper into functional foods and beverages could provide consumers with convenient ways to reap its health benefits.

Cayenne pepper's applications extend beyond the realms of cooking and medicine. Its use in gardening as a natural pesticide and soil amendment showcases its environmental benefits. In personal care, cayenne pepper is being incorporated into hair and skincare products, capitalizing on its stimulating and antioxidant properties. Furthermore, its role in self-defense, through the production of pepper sprays, highlights its practical utility in personal safety.

The surprising and diverse applications of cayenne pepper suggest that its potential is far from fully realized. As research and innovation continue, we can expect to see cayenne pepper finding new and unexpected uses in various industries.

Cayenne pepper holds culinary, cultural and symbolic significance in many societies. Its vibrant red color and fiery heat often symbolize passion, vitality, and strength. In various traditions, cayenne pepper is associated with rituals and celebrations, reflecting its deep-rooted cultural importance.

The future of cayenne pepper in cultural contexts will likely see a continuation of these traditions while also adapting to contemporary practices. The growing interest in culinary tourism and the exploration of global cuisines may further elevate the status of cayenne pepper as a cultural icon.

As the demand for cayenne pepper continues to grow, considerations around sustainable and ethical sourcing become increasingly important. Ensuring that cayenne pepper is cultivated in environmentally friendly and socially responsible ways is crucial for its future. Efforts to support fair trade practices and sustainable farming methods will help protect the livelihoods of farmers and preserve the ecosystems where cayenne pepper is grown.

In conclusion, cayenne pepper's journey from ancient civilizations to the modern world is a testament to its remarkable versatility and enduring popularity. Whether enhancing the flavors of our favorite dishes, providing relief from pain, or serving as a symbol of cultural heritage, cayenne pepper remains a spice that ignites passion and curiosity. As we look to the future, the fiery potential of cayenne pepper continues to burn brightly, and the continued exploration and innovation in the use of cayenne pepper will undoubtedly reveal new and exciting possibilities.

HEALING DIY RECIPES

These recipes harness the potent healing power of cayenne pepper and offer natural alternatives to support health and well-being. However, it is important to remember that natural remedies should complement conventional medical treatments until they can replace them. **Always consult with a healthcare professional before starting any new health regimen.**

Caution:

- Always perform a patch test before using this blend on a larger skin area to ensure you don't have any adverse reactions. Pepper will bring some tingling or heat. That is good.
- Be cautious with the amount of juniper essential oil you use; more drops do not necessarily mean better results and excessive essential oil may cause skin irritation.
- Consult with a health care professional for any severe or persistent arthritis symptoms, as this blend is meant to provide relief and not as a replacement for medical treatment.

Cayenne Pepper for Arthritis Pain Relief

Arthritis Oil

This recipe capitalizes on the anti-inflammatory properties of castor oil and cayenne pepper and pairs it with the soothing effects of juniper oil to create a topical blend that may help relieve arthritis symptoms. Juniper oil is believed to have analgesic and anti-inflammatory properties that can provide comfort. Cayenne pepper is used because it absorbs into muscles and joints.

Ingredients:

- ¼ cup of cold-pressed and hexane-free castor oil
- 5-7 drops of juniper essential oil
- 1 teaspoon of ground cayenne pepper
- A small glass dropper bottle with a lid

Instructions:

1. Start with a clean, dry glass dropper bottle.
2. Carefully measure and pour ¼ cup of cold-pressed and hexane-free castor oil into the bottle.
3. Add 5-7 drops of juniper essential oil to the castor oil. (optional)
4. Add 1 teaspoon of ground cayenne pepper or red pepper flakes
5. Close the bottle tightly and shake it gently to mix the oils thoroughly.
6. Your castor oil anti-inflammatory blend is ready for use.

Applications:

1. Wash and dry the affected area thoroughly before application.
2. Using clean hands, apply 2 teaspoons of the blended oil onto the arthritic joint.
3. Gently massage the oil into the skin using circular motions and wrap.
4. Leave the oil on the skin for at least 30 minutes to allow absorption.
5. For best results, apply this blend daily, preferably before bedtime, to help alleviate arthritis discomfort. Wrap with a leakproof castor oil pack wrap. These are sold everywhere.

This topical application can help reduce arthritis pain by increasing blood flow to the affected areas and reducing inflammation.

Arthritis Oil – Version 2

Ingredients:

- 2 tablespoons of cayenne pepper powder
- 1/2 cup of coconut oil or olive oil
- 1/4 cup of beeswax (optional, for a salve-like consistency)

Instructions:

1. In a double boiler, gently heat the coconut oil and beeswax until melted.
2. Stir in the cayenne pepper powder thoroughly.
3. Allow the mixture to cool slightly, then transfer it to a glass jar.
4. Apply a small amount of the mixture to the affected joints, massaging gently. Use 2-3 times a day.
5. Store the mixture in a cool, dark place.

Cayenne Pepper Gargle for Sore Throat

Cayenne pepper's antimicrobial properties, combined with salt, can help alleviate sore throat by reducing inflammation and killing bacteria.

Ingredients:

- 1/4 teaspoon of cayenne pepper powder
- 1 teaspoon of sea salt
- 1 cup of warm water

Instructions:

1. Mix the cayenne pepper and sea salt in warm water.
2. Gargle the solution for 30 seconds, then spit it out. Repeat 3-4 times a day.
3. Do not swallow the mixture, and rinse your mouth with plain water afterward.

Cayenne Pepper Digestive Tonic

This tonic can stimulate digestion, alleviate indigestion, and promote a healthy metabolism.

Ingredients:

- 1/4 teaspoon of cayenne pepper powder
- 1 tablespoon of apple cider vinegar
- 1 teaspoon of raw honey
- 1 cup of warm water

Instructions:

1. Combine the cayenne pepper, apple cider vinegar, and honey in warm water.
2. Stir well until all ingredients are dissolved.
3. Drink this tonic before meals, once or twice daily.

Cayenne Pepper Cold and Flu Remedy

The heat from cayenne pepper can help clear sinuses, and its antimicrobial properties may assist in fighting off infections.

Ingredients:

- 1/4 teaspoon of cayenne pepper powder
- 1 tablespoon of lemon juice
- 1 teaspoon of raw honey
- 1 cup of hot water

Instructions:

1. Mix the cayenne pepper, lemon juice, and honey in hot water.
2. Sip slowly while the mixture is warm.
3. Drink this remedy 2-3 times a day during cold and flu symptoms.

Cayenne Pepper Balm for Muscle Pain

This balm can help relieve muscle pain and tension by increasing blood flow and reducing inflammation.

Ingredients:

- 2 tablespoons of cayenne pepper powder
- 1/2 cup of coconut oil
- 1/4 cup of shea butter
- 10 drops of peppermint essential oil (optional)

Instructions:

1. Melt the coconut oil and shea butter in a double boiler.
2. Stir in the cayenne pepper powder until fully integrated.
3. Add peppermint essential oil if using.
4. Allow the mixture to cool, then transfer it to a container.
5. Apply the balm to sore muscles, massaging gently. Use as needed.

Cayenne Pepper Sinus Relief Steam

The steam infused with cayenne pepper can help clear sinus congestion and provide relief from sinus headaches.

Caution

Wear a sleep mask to protect your eyes. Keep them closed while steaming.

Ingredients:

- 1/2 teaspoon of cayenne pepper powder
- 1 liter of boiling water

Instructions:

1. Pour the boiling water into a large bowl.
2. Add the cayenne pepper powder to the water.
3. Lean over the bowl with a towel covering your head to trap the steam.
4. Inhale deeply for 5-10 minutes.

Cayenne Pepper Toothache Relief

Cayenne pepper and cloves are both natural pain relievers and can help numb toothache pain temporarily.

Ingredients:

- 1/8 teaspoon of cayenne pepper powder
- 1/8 teaspoon of ground clove powder
- A few drops of olive oil

Instructions:

1. Mix the cayenne pepper powder and clove powder together.
2. Add just enough olive oil to make a paste.
3. Apply the paste directly to the affected tooth using a cotton swab.
4. Leave it on for a few minutes, then rinse your mouth with water.

Here are a few general ideas for Cayenne pepper recipes:

Spicy Sauces and Marinades: Create a homemade hot sauce by combining Cayenne pepper with vinegar, garlic, salt, and other desired spices. Use it as a condiment or as a marinade for meats and vegetables.

Spicy Stir-Fries and Curries: Add Cayenne pepper to stir-fries and curries to bring heat and depth of flavor to the dish. It blends well with ingredients like garlic, ginger, soy sauce, and coconut milk.

Spicy Seasonings and Rubs: Mix Cayenne pepper with other spices like paprika, cumin, garlic powder, and onion powder to create a spicy seasoning blend or rub for grilled meats, roasted vegetables, or popcorn.

Spicy Soups and Stews: Add Cayenne pepper to soups and stews for an extra kick. It can complement ingredients like tomatoes, beans, root vegetables, and meats.

Spicy Chocolate Desserts: Experiment with adding a pinch of Cayenne pepper to chocolate-based desserts like brownies, truffles, or hot chocolate. The heat of the spice can create an interesting contrast with the sweetness of the chocolate.

BONUS:

Cayenne Pepper Anti-Cancer Shot

The combination of cayenne pepper and turmeric has been studied for its potential anti-cancer properties, though more research is needed. This mixture can be used as part of a complementary approach to a healthy lifestyle.

Ingredients:

- 1/4 teaspoon of cayenne pepper powder
- 1 tablespoon of turmeric powder
- 1 tablespoon of raw honey
- 1 cup of warm water

Instructions:

1. Mix the cayenne pepper, turmeric powder, and honey in warm water.
2. Stir well until everything is dissolved.
3. Drink this mixture once daily on an empty stomach.

Dr. ABG's Number One AM Fat-Burning Spice Shot

Ingredients:

- 2oz spring water
- 1 tbsp Raw honey
- 1 tbsp fresh organic lemon juice
- 1 tsp organic ginger (dry ground or fresh)
- 1 dash (1/8tsp) cayenne pepper
- 1 dash Ceylon Cinnamon

Instructions:

Mix. Drink each day, warm or at room temperature, first thing in the morning. This will boost your metabolism.

Safety

When using recipes, it is always recommended to consult your physician. Discuss potential conflicts with any medications you are taking. For example, cayenne pepper may increase bleeding if you are taking blood thinners.

Be a Hero with Your Review

"The best way to find yourself is to lose yourself in the service of others." – Mahatma Gandhi

Think about it. This person is a lot like you, or maybe like you were once upon a time. They're eager to learn, want to make a positive change in their lives, and are searching for the right guidance but not sure where to turn.

My dream is to make *Cayenne Pepper: The History. The Heat. The Health.* a tool for everyone. My whole heart is in this mission. To reach this dream, I need to connect with... everyone.

And this is where you, my dear reader, come into play. Believe it or not, many people decide whether to read a book based on what others say about it. *So, here's my heartfelt request on behalf of those actively seeking natural remedies for health and beauty who haven't met you yet:*

Please consider leaving a review for this book.

It won't cost you a dime, only a minute of your time, but it could make a world of difference for another person looking to enhance their health. Your review might be the key to...

... supporting more small businesses in our communities. ...helping another woman provide for her family. ...empowering someone to find meaningful work. ...assisting another in transforming their life. ...making another person's dream a reality.

Feeling that warm, fuzzy feeling inside? That's the joy of helping. And it's super easy to do - just takes a moment to leave a review.

Simply share your thoughts on the website (Amazon, BarnesandNoble, etc.) where you purchased this book.

If you're excited about making a positive impact on someone's journey toward natural and gentle beauty care, then you're exactly who I'm looking for. **Welcome to the family!**

I can't wait to read your review and hear how this book has helped you to boost your health, eliminate digestive problems, and find relief from pain. A huge thank you from the bottom of my heart. Let's get back to discovering more about cayenne pepper together.

Your biggest cheerleader, Dr. Andrea Blake-Garrett

P.S. - Here's a little secret: when you share something valuable, you become even more valued. **If you know another who would benefit from this book, why not spread the love?**

ABOUT THE AUTHOR

Meet **Dr. Andrea Blake-Garrett**, an accomplished science educator and author in the health and fitness genre. An inspiring wife and mother of twins, she is highly passionate about her work as a health and wellness coach and author. Dr. Blake-Garrett's passion for living a healthier lifestyle was reignited in 2020 when she decided to make the transformational changes necessary to become stronger and live healthier. This resulted in her losing 100 pounds.

Dr. *Blake-Garrett*, respectfully called the Notorious Dr. ABG by staff and clients, holds a number of degrees in science and education and has worked as a science educator, educational consultant, personal trainer, and group fitness instructor. She is the founder and CEO of her company Teamnoexcuses50. Her experience working with clients of all ages and fitness levels has given her valuable insights into the challenges people face when trying to improve their health and wellness. Dr. Blake-Garrett has written 5 books on health and fitness, including:

1. Life! Spice It Up! How To Transform And Heal With 5 Everyday Spices
2. Live Fit & Free For Life: Exercise for Seniors 60+
3. FACIAL FITNESS: Revolutionize Your Self-care with Facial Exercises and Holistic Massage Techniques for Neck and Décolletage.

4. Unlocking the Power of Castor Oil: Your Guide to Natural Beauty and Well-Being.

Her books provide practical advice on everything self-care, including mindset, stress management, living pain-free, and exercise. Dr. Blake-Garrett's writing style is engaging and accessible, making complex health and fitness concepts easy for readers to understand and implement. Her books and leadership have helped countless people achieve their health and fitness goals and live happier, healthier lives. Dr. ABG is looking to re-educate people on the importance of making healthier choices. When she's not writing or training clients, Dr. Blake-Garrett enjoys family time, strength training, gardening, traveling, and trying out new healthy recipes in the kitchen. She believes that health and fitness should be fun and sustainable, and her mission is to help as many people as possible achieve their best selves through education and inspiration. Her enthusiasm and energy are contagious, and books by Dr. Andrea Blake-Garrett are quickly becoming a go-to resource for people looking to think and live healthier and DOMINATE their days!

REFERENCES

Adventist's Precise Answers. "Natural Remedies | Barbara O'Neill | Cayenne Pepper Compress." *YouTube*, 11 July 2022, www.youtube.com/watch?v=YDZgXJbJEjk.

Aishwarya, Akshita, and Akshita Aishwarya. "How Do You Use Cayenne Pepper in Cooking?" *Foodnutra - Online Shop Flavoured Dry Fruits and Premium Spices*, 11 Dec. 2023, www.foodnutra.com/how-do-you-use-cayenne-pepper-in-cooking.

Alexander, Kristy. "Cayenne Pepper Can Help Cure Your Acne and Acne Scars." *Apple Rose Beauty*, 12 Sept. 2015, www.applerosebeauty.com/blogs/nature-and-beauty-meet-big-hearts/63375875-cayenne-pepper-can-help-cure-your-acne-and-acne-scars.

Allarakha, Shaziya, MD. "What Are the Benefits of Cayenne Pepper? 13 Potential Benefits." *MedicineNet*, 7 Jan. 2022, www.medicinenet.com/what_are_the_benefits_of_cayenne_pepper/article.htm.

America, Herb Society Of. "Cayenne Pepper – Herb of the Month." *The Herb Society of America Blog*, 1 Aug. 2021, herbsocietyblog.wordpress.com/2021/08/02/cayenne-pepper-herb-of-the-month.

Anthony, Kiara. "7 Peripheral Neuropathy Natural Remedies." *Healthline*, 26 Mar. 2024, www.healthline.com/health/peripheral-neuropathy-natural-treatments#:~:text=Incorporating%20cayenne%20pepper%20i

n%20your,will%20gradually%20reduce%20neuropathy%20se
nsations.

Benzie, Iris F. F., and Sissi Wachtel-Galor. *Herbal Medicine: Biomolecular and Clinical Aspects, Second Edition.* CRC Press, 2011.

Blake-Garrett, Andrea. *LIVE FIT and FREE FOR LIFE: EXERCISE FOR SENIORS 60+: Targeted Exercises That Will Increase Energy, Improve Balance, Mobility and Strength in 21 Days or Less.* 1st ed., Dr. Andrea Blake-Garrett, 2023, a.co/d/8ozOKyi.

Bode, Ann M., and Zigang Dong. "The Two Faces of Capsaicin." *Cancer Research*, vol. 71, no. 8, Apr. 2011, pp. 2809–14. https://doi.org/10.1158/0008-5472.can-10-3756.

"Cayenne." *Mount Sinai Health System,* www.mountsinai.org/health-library/herb/cayenne#:~:text=Native%20Americans%20have%20used%20cayenne,capsaicin%2C%20which%20helps%20reduce%20pain.

"Cayenne Pepper." *The Epicentre*, 21 Mar. 2020, theepicentre.com/spice/cayenne-pepper.

"Cayenne Pepper Benefits, Nutrition, Uses and Recipes - Dr. Axe." *Dr. Axe*, 1 May 2024, draxe.com/nutrition/cayenne-pepper-benefits.

"Cayenne Pepper: Important Facts, Health Benefits, and Recipes." *relish.com*, 21 July 2023, www.relish.com/food-wiki/153792/cayenne-pepper-important-facts-health-benefits-and-recipes.

Clinic, Cleveland. "Health Benefits of Cayenne Pepper." *Cleveland Clinic*, 27 June 2024, health.clevelandclinic.org/cayenne-pepper-benefits.

Corson, Timothy W., and Craig M. Crews. "Molecular Understanding and Modern Application of Traditional Medicines: Triumphs and Trials." *Cell*, vol. 130, no. 5, Sept. 2007, pp. 769–74. https://doi.org/10.1016/j.cell.2007.08.021.

"Creating Extraordinary Culinary Delights With Cayenne Pepper Ground - Castle Foods." *Castle Foods*, 23 May 2023, castlefoods.com/vault-guide/creating-extraordinary-culinary-delights-with-cayenne-pepper-ground.

Debreceni, Andras, et al. "Capsaicin Increases Gastric Emptying Rate in Healthy Human Subjects Measured by 13C-labeled Octanoic Acid Breath Test." *Journal of Physiology-Paris*, vol. 93, no. 5, Nov. 1999, pp. 455–60. https://doi.org/10.1016/s0928-4257(99)00114-x.

"Does Cayenne Pepper Lower Blood Pressure?" *Quora*, www.quora.com/Does-cayenne-pepper-lower-blood-pressure.

Evans, Hayleigh. "Gardener Shares Ingeniously Simple Hack for Keeping Wildlife Away From Your Plants: 'They'll Bite It Once, but Never Again.'" *The Cool Down*, 29 Dec. 2023, www.thecooldown.com/green-home/cayenne-pepper-garden-hack-squirrels-deer-vermin/#:~:text=To%20repel%20garden%20pests%2C%20this,banish%20woodland%20animals%20and%20bugs.&text=The%20cayenne%20pepper%20hack%20is,few%20weeks%20or%20after%20rainfall.

Farquhar-Smith, Paul, et al. *Landmark Papers in Pain: Seminal Papers in Pain with Expert Commentaries*. Oxford UP, 2018.

Fattori, Victor, et al. "Capsaicin: Current Understanding of Its Mechanisms and Therapy of Pain and Other Pre-Clinical and Clinical Uses." *Molecules*, vol. 21, no. 7, June 2016, p. 844. https://doi.org/10.3390/molecules21070844.

Fenton, Crystal. "7 Benefits of Cayenne Pepper Fruit Extract for Hair." *VEGAMOUR*, 24 Mar. 2024, vegamour.com/blogs/blog/cayenne-pepper-fruit-extract-for-hair.

Flint, Farmer. "Cayenne Pepper Powder: A Culinary Alchemist's Secret Weapon." *FarmerFlints*, 14 Sept. 2023, farmerflints.com/blogs/news/cayenne-pepper-powder-a-culinary-alchemists-secret-weapon.

Fokkens, Wytske, et al. "Capsaicin for Rhinitis." *Current Allergy and Asthma Reports*, vol. 16, no. 8, Aug. 2016, https://doi.org/10.1007/s11882-016-0638-1.

Fox Integrated Healthcare. "Natural Treatments for Neuropathy in Your Legs and Feet." *https://foxintegratedhealthcare.com*, foxintegratedhealthcare.com/neuropathy/natural-treatments-for-neuropathy-in-your-legs-and-feet. Accessed 3 Jan. 2024.

Gevorgyan, Artur, et al. "Capsaicin for Non-allergic Rhinitis." *Cochrane Library*, vol. 2015, no. 7, July 2015, https://doi.org/10.1002/14651858.cd010591.pub2.

Grant, Amy. "Natural Pest Repellent: Do Hot Peppers Deter Pests in the Garden." *Gardeningknowhow*, 9 Sept. 2022, www.gardeningknowhow.com/special/organic/do-hot-peppers-deter-pests.htm.

Green, James. *The Herbal Medicine-Maker's Handbook: A Home Manual*. Crossing Press, 2011.

---. *The Herbal Medicine-Maker's Handbook: A Home Manual*. Crossing Press, 2011.

Guedes, Vânia, et al. "Topical Capsaicin for Pain in Osteoarthritis: A Literature Review." *Reumatología Clínica (English Edition)*, vol. 14, no. 1, Jan. 2018, pp. 40–45. https://doi.org/10.1016/j.reumae.2016.07.013.

Horstermans, Paul. "Cayenne Peppers' Incredible Benefits &Amp; How to Utilise." *En*, 23 Dec. 2023, www.ancientpurity.com/blog/cayenne-peppers-incredible-benefits-how-to-utilise.

---. "Cayenne Peppers' Incredible Benefits &Amp; How to Utilise." *En*, 23 Dec. 2023, www.ancientpurity.com/blog/cayenne-peppers-incredible-benefits-how-to-utilise.

Hultquist, Mike. "Cayenne Peppers - All About Them." *Chili Pepper Madness*, 5 June 2023, www.chilipeppermadness.com/chili-pepper-types/medium-hot-chili-peppers/cayenne-chili-peppers.

Insoles, Vivian Lou Insolia®. "Sore Feet? Spice Things up With Cayenne Pepper!" *Vivian Lou Insolia® Insoles*, www.vivianlou.com/blogs/high-heels-without-the-hurt/63795715-sore-feet-spice-things-up-with-cayenne-pepper.

K, V. Sri Sreshtaa Leslie Rani. S., Brundha M. P, Anjaneyulu. "DIETARY CAPSAICIN AND IMMUNE SYSTEM." *International Journal of Psychosocial Rehabilitation*, 1 Feb. 2020, www.psychosocial.com/article/PR20221102/33628.

Knibbs, Jessica. "Hair Loss Treatment: Cayenne Pepper and Olive Oil Could Increase Hair Growth." *Express.co.uk*, 3 Dec. 2020, www.express.co.uk/life-style/health/1367772/hair-loss-treatment-cayenne-pepper-olive-oil-increase-hair-growth.

Komal, and Komal. "Cayenne 101: Health and Beauty Benefits." *Sweet & Masālā*, 28 Oct. 2016, www.sweetandmasala.com/cayenne-101-health-beauty-benefits.

Lesser, Jennifer. "How to Grow and Care for Cayenne Peppers." *The Spruce*, 2 June 2023, www.thespruce.com/growing-cayenne-pepper-plant-5089794.

Mason, Lorna, et al. "Systematic Review of Topical Capsaicin for the Treatment of Chronic Pain." *BMJ*, vol. 328, no. 7446, Mar. 2004, p. 991. https://doi.org/10.1136/bmj.38042.506748.ee.

Maynard, Jane. "15 Crazy Amazing Things Made Better With Cayenne Pepper." *Cosmopolitan*, 6 July 2022, www.cosmopolitan.com/food-cocktails/a28433/cayenne-pepper-recipes.

Mbbs, Karthik Kumar. "What Cayenne Pepper Does to Your Body: Benefits, Side Effects." *MedicineNet*, 2 May 2024, www.medicinenet.com/what_cayenne_pepper_does_to_your_body/article.htm.

McCarty, Mark F., et al. "Capsaicin May Have Important Potential for Promoting Vascular and Metabolic Health: Table 1." *Open Heart*, vol. 2, no. 1, June 2015, p. e000262. https://doi.org/10.1136/openhrt-2015-000262.

McCormick Science Institute. "Red Pepper | McCormick Science Institute." *McCormick Science Institute*, www.mccormickscienceinstitute.com/resources/culinary-spices/herbs-spices/red-pepper.

Meltzer, Eli O., et al. "Treatment of Congestion in Upper Respiratory Diseases." *International Journal of General Medicine*, Feb. 2010, p. 69. https://doi.org/10.2147/ijgm.s8184.

"Modulation of Select Immune Responses by Dietary Capsaicin." *PubMed*, 1998, pubmed.ncbi.nlm.nih.gov/9565827.

Mutahar, Abdullah Khalil Abdullah. "Health Benefits of Cayenne Pepper - Klarity Health Library." *Klarity Health Library*, 17 Oct. 2023, my.klarity.health/health-benefits-of-cayenne-pepper.

Ngo, Hope. "How to Use Cayenne Pepper to Deal With Pests in Your Garden." *House Digest*, 12 Feb. 2023, www.housedigest.com/1194035/how-to-use-cayenne-pepper-to-deal-with-pests-in-your-garden.

Ody, Penelope. *The Complete Medicinal Herbal*. DK, 1993.

Omolo, Morrine, et al. "Antimicrobial Properties of Chili Peppers." *Infectious Disease & Therapy*, 2014, d1wqtxts1xzle7.cloudfront.net/55740457/important_chilli-libre.pdf?1518020489=&response-content-

disposition=inline%3B+filename%3DAntimicrobial_Propertie
s_of_Chili_Pepper.pdf&Expires=1723848656&Signature=ON
Df7nlwssEkJe2QzvZPEFGv9-
HPyc0kYRASxLsdjrWkFw7aX~AWeu5X1dYW5V1oKwZvy
JrTYtfRug6mKr3FP0Onryjj~hVinxBnUGWpiC7syDjQYrpq
mldGSnpU~u6Mg7Pq-HAZhicJ-
WDBvRBvoG4qTOf6nAUFCcE7GLfgUg3EU7dWKIM4lg20
gU2UjNU3UZNUiStVNqbMUbyv3B19yFivCNnaEl~Tg2Lci
0hSuDIXxPArcfMOI6w9KUBwFYHDahuvbMMtLtpjG4uN8
nYLi6bfx8mrpgcFjcJ2p5wXiiDQdzXgw4isQ7GxgiybpPH1c0
hrtuVYHAvRzYwdwXLipw__&Key-Pair-
Id=APKAJLOHF5GGSLRBV4ZA.

O'Neill, Jessica, et al. "Unravelling the Mystery of Capsaicin: A
Tool to Understand and Treat Pain." *Pharmacological
Reviews*, vol. 64, no. 4, Sept. 2012, pp. 939–71.
https://doi.org/10.1124/pr.112.006163.

---. "Unravelling the Mystery of Capsaicin: A Tool to Understand
and Treat Pain." *Pharmacological Reviews*, vol. 64, no. 4,
Sept. 2012, pp. 939–71. https://doi.org/10.1124/pr.112.006163.

"Oral Capsaicin as Treatment for Unexplained Chronic Cough and
Airway Symptoms." *CHEST Pulmonary*, 20 Mar. 2024,
www.chestpulmonary.org/article/S2949-7892(24)00015-
1/fulltext. Accessed 16 May 2024.

Parsamehr, Farzad, and Farzad Parsamehr. "The History and
Origin of Cayenne Red Pepper." *iSpice You*, 18 Apr. 2023,
www.ispiceyou.com/blogs/news/the-history-and-origin-of-
cayenne-red-pepper.

"Publication Manual of the American Psychological Association (7th Ed.)." *American Psychological Association eBooks*, 2020, https://doi.org/10.1037/0000165-000.

Rd, Jillian Kubala Ms. "6 Potential Health Benefits of Cayenne Pepper." *Healthline*, 1 Feb. 2023, www.healthline.com/nutrition/8-benefits-of-cayenne-pepper.

Roche, N., et al. "Nasal Response to Capsaicin in Patients With Allergic Rhinitis and in Healthy Volunteers: Effect of Colchicine." *American Journal of Respiratory and Critical Care Medicine*, vol. 151, no. 4, Apr. 1995, pp. 1151–58. https://doi.org/10.1164/ajrccm/151.4.1151.

Sayee, Anjali. "Cayenne Pepper for Hair: Benefits, How to Use It and Side Effects." *STYLECRAZE*, 8 May 2024, www.stylecraze.com/articles/cayenne-pepper-help-in-hair-growth.

Shah, Mehak. "Cayenne Pepper: Health Benefits &Amp; Potential Side Effects- HealthifyMe." *HealthifyMe*, 24 June 2022, www.healthifyme.com/blog/cayenne-pepper.

Smith, Howard S. *Current Therapy in Pain*. Elsevier Health Sciences, 2009.

Sylvia. *How to Make Castor Oil and Cayenne Infusion | Sylvia Shackleton Orthotics 2 Go*. orthotics2go.com/how-to-make-castor-oil-and-cayenne-infusion.

Szallasi, Arpad. "The Vanilloid (Capsaicin) Receptor TRPV1 in Blood Pressure Regulation: A Novel Therapeutic Target in Hypertension?" *International Journal of Molecular Sciences*,

vol. 24, no. 10, May 2023, p. 8769.
https://doi.org/10.3390/ijms24108769.

Team, Whatsfordinner. "How to Make Your Meals More
Interesting With Cayenne Pepper." *Whatsfordinner*, 12 July
2023, www.whatsfordinner.co.za/articles/how-to-make-your-
meals-more-interesting-with-cayenne-pepper.

The Real Kitchen. "Member's Mark Cayenne Pepper - the Real
Kitchen." *The Real Kitchen*, 27 July 2022,
therealkitchen.com/product/members-mark-cayenne-
pepper/#:~:text=Organic%20cayenne%20pepper%20is%20an,
applied%20directly%20to%20items%20themselves.

Today, Delaney Nothaft Usa. "Spicy Food Has Health Benefits.
But There Are Some Things You Should Know." *Aberdeen
News*, 21 July 2024, www.usatoday.com/story/life/health-
wellness/2023/08/17/is-spicy-food-good-for-you-immune-
system-weight/70448744007.

Toukan, Nour, et al. "Therapeutic Applications of Capsaicin in
Humans to Target Conditions of the Respiratory System: A
Scoping Review." *Respiratory Medicine*, vol. 194, Apr. 2022,
p. 106772. https://doi.org/10.1016/j.rmed.2022.106772.

WebMD Editorial Contributor. "Health Benefits of Cayenne
Pepper." *WebMD*, 20 Nov. 2023,
www.webmd.com/diet/health-benefits-cayenne-pepper.

White, E. E. "The Spicy Truth: The Unbeatable Duo of Castor Oil
and Cayenne for Neuropathy." *Medium*, 9 Apr. 2024,
astropagan.com/the-spicy-truth-the-unbeatable-duo-of-castor-
oil-and-cayenne-for-neuropathy-6a36a3ba0ee4.

Wikipedia contributors. "Spice Trade." *Wikipedia*, 23 June 2024, en.wikipedia.org/wiki/Spice_trade.

Wilson, Peter, et al. *Clinical Pain Management Second Edition: Chronic Pain*. CRC Press, 2008.

Made in the USA
Columbia, SC
25 September 2024

43006758R00050